BIRDS

designed and written by Althea
illustrated by Veronica Barge

Longman Group USA Inc.

Published in the United States of America by Longman Group USA Inc.
© 1977, 1988 Althea Braithwaite

Originally published in Great Britain in a slightly altered form by Longman Group UK Limited

ISBN: 0-88462-178-2   (library bound)
ISBN: 0-88462-179-0   (paperback)

Printed in the United States of America

88 89 90 10 9 8 7 6 5 4 3 2 1

Library of Congress Cataloging-in-Publication Data
Althea.
   Birds.

   (Life-cycle books/Althea)
   Summary: Describes the nesting, reproduction, and life cycle of the finch.
   1. Birds--Juvenile literature. [1. Finches. 2. Birds] I. Barge, Veronica, ill. II. Title. III. Series: Althea. Life-cycle books.
   QL676.2.A37 1988   598   88-13902
   ISBN 0-88462-178-2 (lib. bdg.)
   ISBN 0-88462-179-0 (pbk.)

Notes for parents and teachers

Life-Cycle Books have been specially written and designed as a simple, yet informative, series of factual nature books for young children.

The illustrations are bright and clear, and children can "read" the pictures while the story is read to them.

The text has been specially set in large type to make it easy for children to follow along or even to read for themselves.

Spring is here.
The female bird listens
to the male bird's song.
Soon they will mate.

The two birds help each other
build a nest.
It is hidden safely in the bushes.

The nest is made from twigs
and lined with feathers and grass
to make it warm and comfortable.

The female bird takes
four days to lay her eggs
in the nest.

She and the male bird
guard the nest.

Small animals and
sometimes snakes
eat bird eggs when
they have the chance.

8

Now the female bird stays
on the nest all the time.
She keeps the eggs warm
so that they will hatch.

The male bird brings her
food because she does not
leave to feed herself.

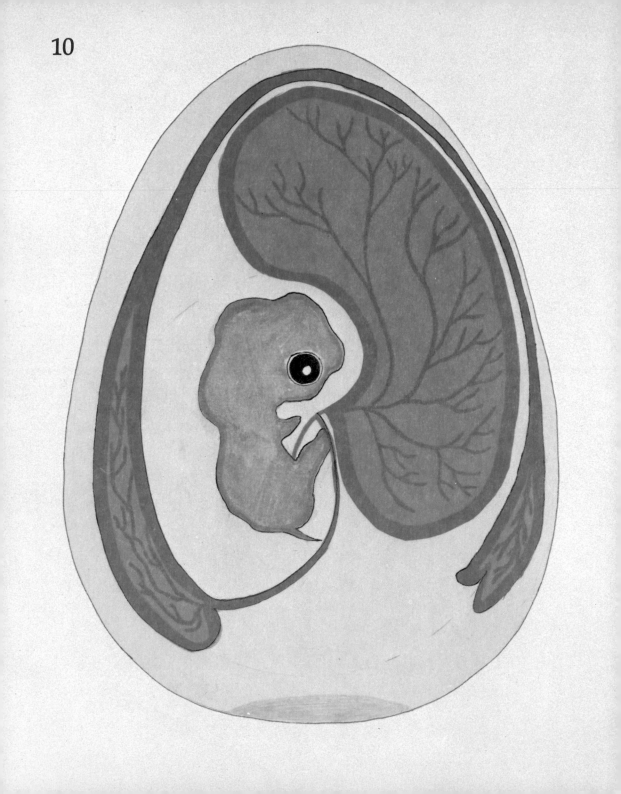

Inside each egg
a baby bird is growing.

At first the baby bird
hardly looks like
a bird at all.
But it soon has eyes and
the beginning of wings,
legs and a tail.

The food the baby bird
needs to grow is stored
in the egg.

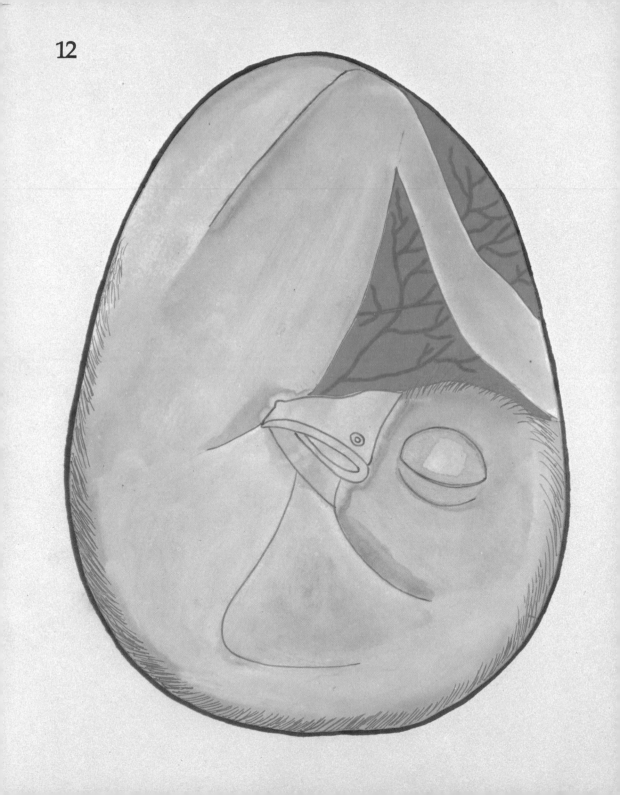

After a few weeks,
the baby is ready
to hatch.

The tiny bird has
used all the food
inside the egg.
It needs to
stretch its body,
open its eyes,
breathe and eat
new kinds of food.

The baby bird pecks
its way out of the eggshell.

Soon there are four little
birds in the nest.
Their beaks look very big.
They have no feathers,
but a soft down
keeps them warm.

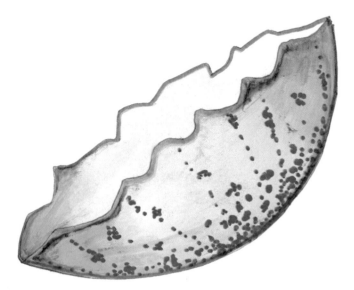

The mother and father birds
are kept very busy feeding
their hungry babies.
The little birds grow fast.
They get stronger and push
one another around.
Each wants to be fed first.

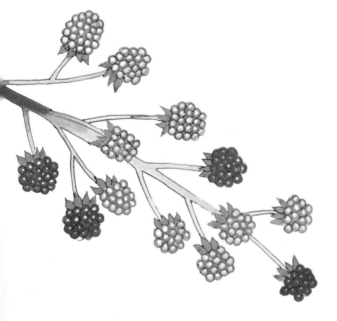

The baby birds are bigger and
have wing feathers.
They must learn to fly.
The parent birds encourage
them to leave the nest.
Fluttering their wings, the babies
land gently on nearby twigs.

Their parents offer them food,
and the babies try to flutter
back to the nest.

Soon they learn to fly
and to feed themselves.

Now the young birds can
look after themselves.
They fly away from the nest.

Perhaps next year they will
find mates and build nests
of their own.

THE BIRDS pictured here are bullfinches, found in Britain and much of Europe. Somewhat larger members of the species are sometimes sighted as "casual migrants" in islands off Alaska.

Goldfinches are perhaps the finches most often seen in North America; the male is easy to identify in the summer with his black cap, bright yellow body, black wing markings and tail.

The American goldfinch is often called a wild canary, but unlike a true canary, its color varies during the year. In the winter it is brownish, and the female is never as bright as the male.

Goldfinches nest in bushes, and live in weedy fields, woods and along waysides. They breed as far north as southern Canada and can be seen year round in much of the United States, although some fly south to winter in the Gulf states and northern Mexico.

Other North American finches are somewhat harder to recognize. All are small birds about the size of English sparrows and white-breasted nuthatches, or about half the size of city pigeons and blue jays—birds usually familiar to children whether they live in the country or an urban area.

Birds in the finch family are mainly seed eaters. Goldfinches are often found in patches of thistle and when sunflower seeds are ripe, feeding on the seed heads.

Finches fly in a dipping, up-and-down pattern, and sometimes flock together. Different finches prefer different locations, some at the forest's edge, others near farms and gardens, in pine forests or among shrubby plants.

Bird-watching is popular, and youngsters led by a knowledgeable adult, armed with a simple bird book, can learn to recognize birds in their area. The National Audubon Society and the National Wildlife Federation are nonprofit organizations that promote conservation and have materials that children as well as adults can use.